I0151341

Wooden Horses

poems by

John Brogan

Finishing Line Press
Georgetown, Kentucky

Wooden Horses

Copyright © 2019 by John Brogan
ISBN 978-1-64662-055-5 First Edition
All rights reserved under International and Pan-American Copyright Conventions.
No part of this book may be reproduced in any manner whatsoever without written
permission from the publisher, except in the case of brief quotations embodied in
critical articles and reviews.

ACKNOWLEDGMENTS

Thank you to...
Victor Mackenzie for the inspiration to write
Betsy and Steve for always being there

Publisher: Leah Maines
Editor: Christen Kincaid
Cover Art: Woodrow W. Cowher
Author Photo: Ettore Fantin
Cover Design: Elizabeth Maines McCleavy

Printed in the USA on acid-free paper.
Order online: www.finishinglinepress.com
            also available on amazon.com

Author inquiries and mail orders:
Finishing Line Press
P. O. Box 1626
Georgetown, Kentucky 40324
U. S. A.

Table of Contents

I. Family

★ ★ ★

Timshel

We were all ill prepared, a slim stem
rootless in firm ground; the door
opens on life without a sound, leaving debris
to piece together unknown realms.

Newborn, he grabbed for a flower,
and we as parents wonder in what ways
the petals will tear; as he grazes through days
what will he say is the story of his tower?

Transitions are doors to gated daffodil beds,
where foreseers, sprouting in Eden's den, say
"Welcome to a piece of life!" Whose aim
is to discover sense—a drive to ascend.

Friday Night with My Son

Your soft plum skin is so frail
From your newly rooted seeds
In tree-city's war-patched trails
Where buckeyes brew into mead.

Sleep thoroughly and gentle,
You elemental lentil,
A ruminating kettle—
Bean root, life's newest renter.

Sleep with Open Eyes

Wake loudly with a little version of life!
Sleep with open eyes like a fruit bat—
Be careful not to bathe in the glooms of life,
They sting like a thief's knife in the dark mat
Of night; be the soldier flying with remark
Over enemy sites, soaring with epithet wings
Past trenches, toward richer embarks!
Your first vocal chords already sing of dreams.

Bonds of atoms that make up tree branch arcs
Create great vantage points to see through seams.
Always keep open eyes, even while stark asleep;
Your first vocal chords already sing of dreams.

The Tiger Is Left to Find His Wings

The tiger is like a young boy who
In an instant realizes he went down
The slide too fast (slippery from dew),
Unprepared for the thrilling letdown.

This tiger prowls to find his wings
Between tangles of bent kindling
And dense brush that tingle
His fur, which is exciting and new.

This tiger cries for his parents, already
Out of his mind, eager for it all—
The parents can't stop thorns from pecking,
Just as they can't choose where leaves fall.

This tiger is eager to bring on the day
And opens his mitts to stretch his paws,
Like a man uses his hand to cover his yawn,
Crying but not hiding from the wild.

Let Him Jump

Never wake a sleeping baby or else
He may lose growing neuron cells;
The climber breaks from his laminated stable
Like a cracked aquarium, ecstatic to tell

That rain is flying sideways from the south;
Behind window panes and Dow
TV screens; in town thunder is a welcome
Sound, rain in summer being so rare.

Leaving the stable with electrified hands,
In the weatheredness it is difficult to attain
Comfort, but the rain's smell helps; he goes
To the river with nothing but a basket of twine.

The horsepower of his climb amounts
To thundering through overgrown pines,
His destination a shoreline that ticks,
Slowly flowing like blue blood.

Never prevent a will to climb where boarders
Mark territories, even if to feel fear dissolve,
Like when a little hand clasps a finger
Even if it will one day throw it away.

Wrapped in history's embrace, like
A newborn swaddled in a relative's
Quilt that is now a relic (but also nothing),
The climber sees the river flowing fast.

Name on the Wall

Like a fly on the wall, time is quiet,
Known as the moth out at night;
He pounced through fire that smells
Like raining cement and drying water.

Had he ever thought of the house dog
As rebar to concrete? Rather a tamed beast
Than a puppy mill screech; new breeds
Don't need associated names.

The quieter it is, the louder wolves howl—
The lucky get plastic and steel houses
But still'd rather kids in by dark
Well before hearing growls or barks.

It's ominous to be awake after four
But cleansing to be up before five;
You wake up to whatever alarm
Crosses by with its dog leash.

Liquidity to your investments
Is longevity to your name, we
Think of it as permanent
But disintegration is always in mind.

Naming your blue-rich blood
Is a way to test lineage; showing
Liquidity in time stops, despite
Time running its pass; yet circumstances

Of each birth make it that
Every name has four or five behind it
Prowling in the night as the kids
Wonder why it's all strange.

Algae on the Lake

Doves fly overhead, eyeing the man's bread
Being tossed in pieces to the lake where pigeons
Flock over discarded TVs playing nature films
On the Great Lakes and the troubles they face.

Algae blooms similar to Scooby-Doo characters....
Sea urchins sneaking along shores
Of the mainland: industry retaliation—
Conquering is humanity fully realized.

On a photograph in the servant's back pocket
Is a family, while a sea of doves fly overhead
For their crumbs, knowing they've seen what life is
By having been present and alive.

If we are lucky to drop an heirloom from
The stork as it bats away the pigeons and doves
Clinging to their TV sets and Pepsi products
Then we are blessed to live along with Scooby-Doo

Monsters and new Coke flavors before the crows call
And selected pallbearers must throw you into water
To sleep with algae and 90s' broken TV sets
Alongside family men tossing bread to the birds.

The Wind Rolling along a Home

Slow music please, the world won't cease
while winds crash against snowy
lashes of lakeside attractions laced in ice.

Overnight frozen waves peel over cars,
as if water was a once-living animal, its pelt
decorative for a taxidermist's belt—
or leftover shaving cream after a fresh cut.

As the sun comes out to illuminate
remains of a snowstorm the night previously,
(Tchaikovsky-like in its delivery)
the wind rolls along the shore
like slow melodies in a hallucinating memory.

A holiday morning to stay warm in,
radiating a frenetic musical pleasure
as time moves forward with the wind rolling
toward a new year in slow measure,
yet with an elastic intensity
to match the intentions of a family.

Light the Way to Push the Waves

Skyscraper light towers
Put anyone in awe; the view…
Thanks to the moon there are
Mighty crashes along their seams.

Won't you be the skyscraper looking
Out into a chaos of bubbling sheaths?
Giving solace to the shattering shoreline,
Crushing foam like a blanket sheet.

Comfort the world with light
For in its vastness the world is sick;
Let your gaze blind onlookers
Who thought they could handle the sea.

Let blackberries grow along your seams,
To fend off the things of life lost to fear—
Light the way for the moon
To push the waves.

Hand You the Sky

Kaleidoscope stars encircle
the moon's caressing curves,
highlighting its star-dusted peaks
and deafening its craters.

I drove you there in a storm
while you rejected tears away.
Beauty is quite OK and demands
only beautiful responses; there
are no immovable walls in space.

Mars rotates while we float above,
under colliding stars whose
reflections dance along your seams.

You're cold, I'm shivering,
we must be dead.
An IV won't be able to
force our bodies to solid ground.

The wind is pulsating past our
bleeding feet, our entire bodies
touching and pumping blood through
our veins, while the stars make
the air look like crystals
and rubies dancing along an autumn lake.

There's no coming down my dear,
it's so late that it's a new morning.

A touch of your love
and now I'm blind!
I'm on a hill going blind,
so quick, hurry to
accept as I hand you the sky.

Moments Outside the Fragment

"All this jackery from outlandish penury
Helps account for history in its most raw,
But why should that mean we stay stagnant?
I can't stand being a fragment."

"To sear the ego from your fragment
Must be a talent, in many respects,
But leaves a subsequent contempt,
As if a rejected lover keeps coming back."

"You speak in nonsense—let's go on a trip!
Your shoulders are tense, even after that slip
Of whiskey in your coffee...
You noticed I could tell and did nothing."

"Never mind your assumptions,
History tells us our fragments follow us,
Perspective a restraint—on vacation you become a
reduction, to them a fragment elsewhere shaped."

"Your view of the world is boorish.
History tells me it's nice to get away,
Forget your own eyes for a day;
Museum paintings become less contemptuous."

"You fear letting your ego go for neutrality's sake,
But I know how you sleep after makeup sex—
My legs feel open, I think I'll take these off and go into the pool.
I'm bored of perspective...in the water, my sight is fading."

"You sexualize, fetishize our fragments for a voyage,
Seek-and-destroy style—raid the village, hunt for the
Fruitful treasures. We dance with our hips touching
To divide our time into indiscrete pieces."

"I happily divide my time into indiscriminate pieces.
You must let your periphery fade, jump in!
Watch how I swim....Your body is taking over?
Run your wet hands across my lips."

"You're soft and tender, dizzyingly shaped—
I still persist ecstasy is a trick to rid human-ness.
Nature mistakenly let us reflect—we are interpreters—
Now I question my senses even while grasping you."

"Escape! Your insecurity toward life has made you its slave.
Come close, look in my eyes, if you can't be blind to your ego
Then let it become animal... Watch your eyes roll back, slow slow,
How high are you now? Your periphery is fading."

Vacation Is Over for Good

The vacation is over,
once rolling in dogbeds, tolling
in stride to a drum beat
lost to strings and neat clams.

It's over now, the sun
is warm still but similar runs
line its waves like fishy eyes
too long strained in a world long tried.

The vacation is over and rotted,
the dog is dead and gutted,
long ago the belly blood was warm
at night, now cold and decayed.

Two knives in each eye of the damn dog
must have hurt, but death smogs
pain and is silent and nothing,
no laughter left for coming.

The vacation is over,
and the ride was covered
in itching along the way,
the house dog is always rotting.

With the Strength of a Composer

"The strict image of the long-dead composer
Misleads of her true intentions!"
Out of a mossy grove that undoes her.

Antlers pierce the haze to arouse her,
Relieving a lonely secession
Building with the strength of a composer.

A rapid fire leaves its haze of hair, long,
Pathless in the ash (though nothing is askew)
Out of a mossy grove that undoes her.

The forest fire leaves bare logs
To sharpen antlers with as spring starts anew,
Building with the strength of a composer.

The strict image recedes and toggles
As the fire burns in a lustful hue
Out of a mossy grove that undoes her,
Building with the strength of a composer.

The World Is Disorganized

The universe, with no end,
      Lacks a point of understanding
            Though scars always seek one to mend;
      Fanning fires only keeps a base-tan—
Recognizing disorder is to eat death.

            As square shapes are lost trying
      To decide where their lines are,
The charcoal pines (like broken eggs)
      Are dying to be whole,
            To be the sun, an adored star.

            Barbaric, bizarre; with no end—
      Like a vulture's well-spent time,
there's one True Word to record,
      (A crease in the fold that holds it all);
            Maggots live lives most explored.

Eating death, now that's a line
      With three others that can
            Be called a square; there's no end
      To any one point of reasoning,
So the savvy eat death all the time.

Basement Staircase

The body is a field of exploration,
though their foundations chip away
in constant decay; rafters penetrate
our crutches of sense, sealing the breeze.

The attics stay polished though
worn from day after day;
structural beams shake to confide
this is all a temporary dream.

Draw bare the crumbling stairs!
Shovel five feet under the wet musty
dirt, building up vacant anthills
just to kick them back down.

The sixth stair is a basement, painted
white like cloud nine, far from stair five.
The soil underneath is rich and fair,
inescapable, always too near.

Plywood Canoes in a Flood

Two canoes run into white froth, maintaining
Rhythm from engorged raindrops passing by.
Squirrels scurry up high, barely containing
Their wonder as flooding waters topple the pines.

Vibrations from thunder and raging waves
Push the canoes broadside with wind,
Thunking over shallow rocks, their interlocutors
Maintaining an intimated path in the hills.

Grass on higher grounds snake with the wind
Through farm hill contours as if schools of fish;
Hills seem grand nostalgically but can be bland;
The flood at the basin brings on the thrills.

Gliding like cavalry, clanking shields, archers,
Plywood board-bound captains rev like horsemen
As the boys whoa them horses, wagering
Who will win the stakeout when the levee breaks.

Driftwood canoes, once plywood ramps
For bikes and boards when the sun was wooed—
It's all for the thrill. A boy can kill for it,
The chill of flying in the night.

His Father Never Yelled

He never heard his father yell
When the gates were open
When the demons ripped from hell

His frustration like a dope fiend
Leaving a man in desperation
But to come apart isn't the water to quell

I saw a fragment of your vision
In a mild midday conversation
When the demons ripped from hell

I lifted my voice in discontent
Waiting to release tension in a fight
But to come apart isn't the water to quell

Not one purposed to flattery
Truths more ripe than spin
When the demons rip from hell

You later told me you never heard
Your father yell, and that day you were calm
When the demons ripped from hell
And to come apart was not the water to quell

II. Work

★ ★ ★

Some Say there Is a Golden Ladder

Some say there is a golden ladder—
It's secretly discussed by the press.
No paper covers or flatters,
As though the point should be put to rest.
Those who wrote of holy sin captured
What was told to the masses in jest
Since angels, weary of the Rapture,
Fled quick—mortality a failed test.
The laborers stuck to fight capture,
Sharpening blades for unholy raids
In attempts to destroy the ladder.
It's said that those who've seen the flavors
At the top get rid of what matters
Since the rungs were their only savior.

Some say a boy once saw the structure,
Rushed to it, eager for splendor,
To find the ladder a render,
Practically a mirage with gold paint.
The top was boarded, though looked tender,
As if welcomed just if worth the rank.
These stories insist that the papers
Know the ladder is stained-over rust;
That capturers need a long line
So someone's always behind.
A line has order like ladder rungs,
Keeping big eyes small, unrewindable.
Some say there is a golden ladder
Always a fingertip away.

Desert Billboards

Between adjacent walls of capitalized shapes
is pavement—roads we create
to capture the view, forfeiting riskier stakes;
agreeing to billboards for a car path that is safe.

In accordance with pirates throwing loot overboard
(and although mountain time is still), gold—like rebar
in cement, is plastered to the molded seafloor,
and is a picture-in-time's wily keyboard.

Richer lands may not be greener—golden
silhouettes of sand dance in circles from winds
that cover signs, and remind travelers
that billboards are not on mountain time.

An Idle Fame

An idle fame rests on the mantle, rewritten to be
gawked at under eyes of herded cattle
who as a mass are only to engage in idle chatter.

The idle fame is sprawled on a picturesque wooden T,
with a bandolier sketched over, hanging across his ribs
like a rosary dangles under a shrine of glowing candles.

Like sheep to slaughter, the crowd is only vaguely
aware of a larger show, bull's-eye-bound arrows
with unknown targets (spectacles invite silences).

Night's eve to the garden after the fall has been revised
to cater to the needs of thrones; rewritten by restless classes
is a story set ablaze, urging violence within the masses.

Sunrise Sliding like Sand

All night I waited for the sound of red—
eyes foggy,
plopping in frozen fruit to wed
hot tea
with bloodshed red strawberry seeds,
making mush.

The rosary moves in my hand
like hot sand,
Gliding along ripple-shaped landscapes,
callousing
while the moon sways blue, up and high,
violently.

Jolting away from the blue glare—
quickly, jeez!
My sandy red hands glide to find
Any shade,
covering my burnt eyes and skin
from the raid.

Blue moon in your eyes, I see that
in your birth,
you were boiled in frozen fruit,
left over
to spill your guts through finger slits:
morning sun.

Look, forget the parole, the matter
persists
like a thorn in your damaged paw;
goddamn it,
all night I viewed the cold blue moon
to see the harsh sun.

Nighttime Chess

A 12-year-old boy is playing chess at the bar.
Late-night couples whisper about the time—
(The shop manager is happy for his company).

The boy moves his pawn, considering board placement
Over the general landscape of the battlefield,
Wanting the center while maintaining a strong back.

He hears shields crashing and sees blood
Squirting through helmet eye-holes while horses
Trample and the bishops cast blame on the living.

He feels the chilled glass pieces slide across the field
As blood pumps behind his eyes, unsure but thrilled
For the kill—the ultimate win being a will to fight.

The Musician

Salivating at the mouth—
Reached by envelopes of chaos,
Births congestive passions in signals
Resolved by thrusts of
The musical chord;
Jazz never died it was classic.
A culmination of two or
More identities, we call it art
In a nonacademic sense.

Be a Poet

if u want to be a musician
            be a poet

if u seek rhythm in
            otherwise agitable feet
be a poet

if u see colors
as convexed by sight
            be a poet

if u want good company
                  b e a p o e t

if u want a l o v e i n y o u r life
            be a poet

if u see aloneness in being
            as a synonym
of inevitability
            be a poet

            (un) -fortunately
poets are d e a d

fMRI Dream Sequence

Yesterday's dreams
Think about unconditionally
Tomorrow's ratty clothes
The stores are all closed
Put 'em in the magnet
Watch the blood flow
Tell 'em why
Things hate to be alone

Cut the lights
Wipe the sterilized floor
Salesman knocks on the door
The auditor's found a problem
The bill's shaping up too small
The pills are all gone
Put 'em in the magnet

Adult meanings tense to hold
Events are scrambled
They say time is fabric
A set number of materials
Put 'em in the magnet

Things claim to be as they seem
Put 'em in the magnet
Watch the blood flow
Tell 'em why
Things hate to be alone

Circus at Day One

The opossum's a swingin' on a branch
In boredom an' is a pissin' in a pot
(As its gotten so swell at doin')
Quite talented to do in tandem;

And in his peckish attentiveness he's
Learned to enjoy the simple things
Like growin' his bladder til it'll burst
Just for some sweet release;

Thinkin' he'll a piss on the glass between
Them gawkers gawkin' at
His piss and his swingin' and I bet
They like watchin' they don't mind at all;

Oh! How they want to watch a monkey
Piss into a bucket from an impressive distance
While swingin' in circles with cracked-up eyes
Cause it's a circus here right at day one.

Poetry Is Constant, Sometimes Written

Old age midnight bears fruit, despite
A microscope's need to magnify microscopic
Moments; the nearby church chimes
Moan midnight, ringing tinnitus bells
With its constancy, like the point
Where metals collide and travel, like midnight.

Workmen wander paved streets like
Midnight, and ringing bells follow the moon,
Though through a microscope the moon
Is a rock that doesn't move and is
Considered such. Getting home is enough,
Forgotten ringing by shouting and singing
Or signing into debts with goose bumps.

In the technician's vast petri dish
Molecules collide, apparently to bear
Fruit in the sun, but we don't see
These things in real time and trust
Midnight, who in his old age stands still.

Through ringing ears, the scope must need
More micro or none, the view static
And unclear; old age midnight stands still
As the moon does from close up,
Building up the words for the bells to chime.

Catchphrase for the Dead

I'll be damned if

blank walls eat flowers.
   (I'll be damned)
Pledge allegiance to you
lackluster labor
            —the road between home.

Damn

to hell with your words.
Cenobite, the elaborate reversal...
   (carryover art)
—a slice of bread unched in a ball.

(Till death we separate)

Covet the flag tied to the wall,
an enticing show
   (asked to dance along)
with the wind plugged into the wall.

Damn It to Hell

Emphatic negation of nature...
   (aesthetics is a beautiful chamber)
      birth painted red, white, and blue.

A Garden of Blue Dots

A pale blue dot that reflects nothing,
(like two darkened pupils catching
stardust in their paths of sight)
has existed briefly, maybe only seconds.

Genesis lines its nerves: charged
passageways flow like nostrils
breathing in the Holy Spirit;
not to hinder growth, to give it at all.

Eternity lasts like a nuptial feast
overtaken by fierce imperial forces,
insisting old rituals vulgar:
that the current say shape the universal.

Voices on a pale blue dot tend the
growing stems that pierce the dirt
in memory that april brings may,
as stardust circles like rain.

America's Newest Son

America's newest son, who thought
About taking the north-country train
When his rambling was brought
To a panic, went with a plane.

Thinking less of the rising sun's plot,
More of tomorrow's pain,
He stares into the clouds drinking arak,
Eyeing constellations over Spain.

When feeling heartless, he hides from sparkles
But in the sky over the Atlantic, he is warm,
Imagining the first Spanish ships as remarkable,
Though today the direction of his future is torn.

In his window, water is replaced by darkness;
Fly fish are shaped like expanding stars.
His vision brings on a slight illness,
His arms grow red and porous like Mars.

The stars are a scene of misshaping schools
Churning through darkness with space gills
As the sun murmurs of science's rules—
The plane is space bound as far as he can tell.

He turns his head east to the shored land
Condemning it as a misguided mistress,
Claiming the ocean as the mainland,
Owing to its likeness with space's distance.

He wonders if his drinks were a good idea,
The plane is spinning around in circles
Like a teenager's first shot of tequila—
The ocean must be something universal.

To Work or Jail

Who can describe time on the wall
Better than paint drying down the halls?
Maintenance to follow the rules,
To pay the bills—time is cruel.
Clock in and out while hazelnuts fall—
The cold front makes paint congeal well.
There is a clock that minutes the still
Photograph on the desk in the stay
Where slick checks dish out the greenest lawns.
Though social security is tall
The sense of lingering and stalling
Persists like white-water paddlers
Who've lost their way looking at the sky.

Beast of Deep Blue Summits

Solemn mountains slow dance
With the tide, as it licks the neck
Of a mature shoreline whose moans
Are like weathered leaves—sand
As it melts into a castle of rock.

My hands smell like bird beaks
That have been pecking on
Doorbells that ripple river rings; which
Is to say crude, animal, loving.

Romance euphemizes pure ecstasy,
Less to do with remorse or culture,
Such as maybe a baby pooping
On its own midsummer front lawn.

Ghost scripts on tattered leaves
Look like Pollock dreams—
Remember how the trees
Looked from underwater?

The beast is a mountain peak, making
Cheeks red from a cold essence
Lasting longer than passion stabs, which
Is to say it is dull, tepid, alive.

Moan from your bedroom gut
You giant beast that prowls
In the deep-blue summits—
Little known of by design,
Behemoth beyond compare.

The Pale Pill of Summertime

The pillars arrange themselves beforehand,
as they generally seem to respect.
Woodpeckers are busy in these wetlands,
while nearby a frozen riverbank intersects
with hail that the icy channel deflects.

There is a tree-laden trail with rooted stairs,
that in each unrecognizable step needlessly
changes the young forest air
into something more rare, and is a dim frequency.

As I listen for the flowing stream in a mild breeze,
not hearing back from a winter freeze feels rigid—
like a cold syringe buried intravenously
into the most visible bend under a bridge.

When the ice of the bank expanded wide
and there were no reflections in the icy stream's sky
I asked the river, "Why in summer are you cold and dry?"
The result was pale, neither bright nor dark:

in a vision of wisdom atop a mound of dirt,
the river foresaw ripe fruit dying on an industrial land
as the nectar of nature's passions were clumsily
crumpled into back pockets by each passersby
without care, far too many times.

The World of Wild Animals

Distinct regions with unique branching faunas
Scatter and take stake in gene pools staggered,
Differentiating plausible comparisons into a sauna
Of cesspools—granted in a sense of saga;
The tip of the iceberg gallantly daunts along
Like shifting plates leaving treasures in the raw,
Raking soil to expose her bare of her matter
As our trash enters her womb, a baby to rock.

She could never be said to be pure of failure
As the term only exists in mind; genes are padlocked
From its fauna as the pool delineates regular
And gradual changes, as the wild is a preferred stock.

Rolling Waves of Blackbirds

Rolling waves, like a longing wink,
rest on a tempered sunrise's wake.
Blackbirds swarming in droves call on
names of long-forgotten origin stories.

A Darwinian epic of animism, that
while reading spreads like stretching palms,
they fly; each rigid, petrified digit
fluttering in an oblique symmetry.

In the sunrise that is warm,
warmth can be felt only at
some patient and gradual distance,
embodied in a flock of repetition.

An archaeological record, soaring off
in this second, mirrors a time before.
The tendency of anatomical features...
foam in the rolling waves.

www.ingramcontent.com/pod-product-compliance
Lightning Source LLC
LaVergne TN
LVHW051610080426
835510LV00020B/3219